IN THIS ISSUE:

I0393419

ISSUE 02 FEBRUARY 2017

PUBLISHER
Tourism Tattler (Pty) Ltd.
PO Box 891, Umhlanga Rocks, 4320
KwaZulu-Natal, South Africa.
Website: www.tourismtattler.com

EXECUTIVE EDITOR Des Langkilde
Cell: +27 (0)82 374 7260
Fax: +27 (0)86 651 8080
E-mail: editor@tourismtattler.com
Skype: tourismtattler

MAGAZINE ADVERTISING
ADVERTISING DIRECTOR Bev Langkilde
Cell: +27 (0)71 224 9971
Fax: +27 (0)86 656 3860
E-mail: bev@tourismtattler.com
Skype: bevtourismtattler

SUBSCRIPTIONS
http://eepurl.com/bocldD

BACK ISSUES (Click on the covers below).

▼ JAN 2017	▼ DEC 2016	▼ NOV 2016
		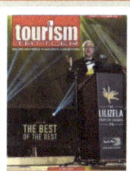

▼ OCT 2016	▼ SEP 2016	▼ AUG 2016

▼ JUL 2016	▼ JUN 2016	▼ MAY 2016

▼ APR 2016	▼ MAR 2016	▼ FEB 2016

CONTENTS

EDITORIAL COMMENT
04 Tourism Safety Communication in South Africa

BUSINESS & FINANCE
06 The Role of Tour Operators in Safari Bookings
08 SATSA Market Intelligence Report
09 Tourism Business Index Q4 2016

CONSERVATION
10 Recording Wildlife Spotting Online

DESTINATIONS
12 The A-B-C's of Réunion Island
14 Exploring Sri Lanka from Tangle to Galle

EVENTS
16 Join the Global Blog-It Influencer Summit
17 Middle East's 'The Hotel Show' Brand Launches in Africa

HEALTH & WELLNESS
18 Tips on How to De-stress

HOSPITALITY
20 Property Profile: Selborne Golf Estate, Hotel and Spa
22 The Old-school General Manager

HUMAN RESOURCES
23 Mobile Images & Employee Privacy

LEGAL
24 The Law: Contracts - Part 26
25 Adventure Tourism from a Legal Perspective - Part 8

NICHE TOURISM
26 Food Tourism: How to Get your Slice of the Pie

TRANSPORT
28 Vehicle Review: Mazda2 Hazumi

Read daily tourism & hospitality news on our Trade News portal

EDITORIAL CONTRIBUTORS

Adam Jacot de Boinod	Kagiso Mosue
Desmond Langkilde	Louis Nel
Erik Wolf	Martin Janse van Vuuren
Fiona Leppan	Romy Toussaint
Guy Stehlik	Tessa Buhrmann

MAGAZINE SPONSORS

06 Lalibela Private Game Reserve	**17** The Hotel Show Africa
12 Réunion Island Tourism Board	**20** Selborne Golf Estate, Hotel and Spa

ACCREDITATION

Official Travel Trade Journal and Media Partner to:

The Africa Travel Association (ATA)
Tel: +1 212 447 1357 • Email: info@africatravelassociation.org • Website: www.africatravelassociation.org

ATA is a division of the Corporate Council on Africa (CCA), and a registered non-profit trade association in the USA, with headquarters in Washington, DC and chapters around the world. ATA is dedicated to promoting travel and tourism to Africa and strengthening intra-Africa partnerships. Established in 1975, ATA provides services to both the public and private sectors of the industry.

The African Travel & Tourism Association (Atta)
Tel: +44 20 7937 4408 • Email: info@atta.travel • Website: www.atta.travel

Members in 22 African countries and 37 worldwide use Atta to: Network and collaborate with peers in African tourism; Grow their online presence with a branded profile; Ask and answer specialist questions and give advice; and Attend key industry events.

National Accommodation Association of South Africa (NAA-SA)
Tel: +27 86 186 2272 • Fax: +2786 225 9858 • Website: www.naa-sa.co.za

The NAA-SA is a network of mainly smaller accommodation providers around South Africa – from B&Bs in country towns offering comfortable personal service to luxurious boutique city lodges with those extra special touches – you're sure to find a suitable place, and at the same time feel confident that your stay at an NAA-SA member's establishment will meet your requirements.

Regional Tourism Organisation of Southern Africa (RETOSA)
Tel: +27 11 315 2420/1 • Fax: +27 11 315 2422 • Website: www.retosa.co.za

RETOSA is a Southern African Development Community (SADC) institution responsible for tourism growth and development. RETOSA's aims are to increase tourist arrivals to the region through. RETOSA Member States are Angola, Botswana, DR Congo, Lesotho, Madagascar, Malawi, Mauritius, Mozambique, Namibia, Seychelles, South Africa, Swaziland, Tanzania, Zambia and Zimbabwe.

Southern African Vehicle Rental and Leasing Association (SAVRALA)
Contact: manager@savrala.co.za • Website: www.savrala.co.za

Founded in the 1970's, SAVRALA is the representative voice of Southern Africa's vehicle rental, leasing and fleet management sector. Our members have a combined national footprint with more than 600 branches countrywide. SAVRALA are instrumental in steering industry standards and continuously strive to protect both their members' interests, and those of the public, and are therefore widely respected within corporate and government sectors.

Seychelles Hospitality & Tourism Association (SHTA)
Tel: +248 432 5560 • Fax: +248 422 5718 • Website: www.shta.sc

The Seychelles Hospitality and Tourism Association was created in 2002 when the Seychelles Hotel Association merged with the Seychelles Hotel and Guesthouse Association. SHTA's primary focus is to unite all Seychelles tourism industry stakeholders under one association in order to be better prepared to defend the interest of the industry and its sustainability as the pillar of the country's economy.

International Coalition of Tourism Partners (ICTP)
Website: www.tourismpartners.org
ICTP is a travel and tourism coalition of global destinations committed to Quality Services and Green Growth.

International Institute for Peace through Tourism
Website: www.iipt.org
IIPT is dedicated to fostering tourism initiatives that contribute to international understanding and cooperation.

ITB Asia 2017
Website: www.itb-asia.com
25 to 27 October 2017 Marina Bay Sands®, Singapore.
ITB Asia is the leading B2B travel trade event for the entire Asia-Pacific region.

Tourism, Hotel Investment and Networking Conference 2017
Website: www.thincafrica..com
THINC Africa 2017 takes place in Cape Town, South Africa from 6-7 September.

The Hotel Show Africa 2017
Website: TheHotelShowAfrica.com
Thousands of hospitality professionals from around the world will be at Gallagher Convention Centre in Johannesburg from 25-27 June.

The Safari Awards
Website: www.safariawards.com
Safari Award finalists are amongst the top 3% in Africa and the winners are unquestionably the best.

World Luxury Hotel Awards
Website: www.luxuryhotelawards.com
World Luxury Hotel Awards is an international company that provides award recognition to the best hotels from all over the world.

Global Travel Blogger & Influencer Summit
Website: www.blogit.travel
September 26-28, 2017, INDIA. Blog IT is an annual gathering that provides an opportunity for attendees and speakers to network.

Tourism Safety Communication in South Africa

A focussed public-private partnership approach for the South African tourism industry to positively inform potential visitors on safety and security issues is imperative for the country to compete as a safe destination on the global tourism stage. Here's the Who, What, Why and How – what's missing is the When.

By **Des Langkilde**.

Search the web using the title of this article as keywords and you will find that the top results deliver negative advice regarding the country, primarily emanating from travel advisory websites such as gov.uk (alarmingly, the UK is one of South Africa's key inbound markets), USA Today and TripAdvisor.

Negative terms such as rape, crime, murder, vehicle hijacking, robbery, ATM fraud, and luggage theft predominate. USA Today starts its 'Travel Tips' advisory with: *"High violent crime and murder rates have earned South Africa a reputation as a dangerous destination..."*

And local travel websites are no better. An analysis of eight South African public sector tourism websites that deal with safety issues shows that in most instances warnings are phrased in a negative manner, i.e. "do not". In many cases, the safety and security information is hidden behind other information aimed at marketing the destination. With the exception of the provision of emergency numbers, virtually no advice exists on how to respond to various types of victimisation. In other words – if you have been a victim of card fraud, follow these steps, or if you had your passport stolen, then these are the steps to follow.

The author of the above analysis, Ian van Vuuren – Project Consultant, Tourism Safety Initiative (TSI), Tourism Business Council of South Africa (TBCSA), suggests a focussed public-private partnership approach for the South African tourism industry to ultimately achieve the following:

- Develop a common "macro" message that can be replicated at national, provincial and city levels.
- From this generic message, more specific messages may be developed by local authorities, tourism product owners and service providers.
- These messages should in all cases phrase matters, as far as is possible, in a positive manner, i.e. "do" instead of "do not".
- Links would be provided for support of various types on all sites, i.e. emergency responders, trauma councillors, translators, embassies, banks, etc.
- Develop common ways to respond to specific types of emergencies.
- These messages should be developed in a "fun" manner, i.e. interactive colourful posters that integrate normal tourism information with safety and security information in a seamless manner.

In the final analysis, van Vuuren concludes that "What is required to counter negative perceptions of South Africa as a tourist destination

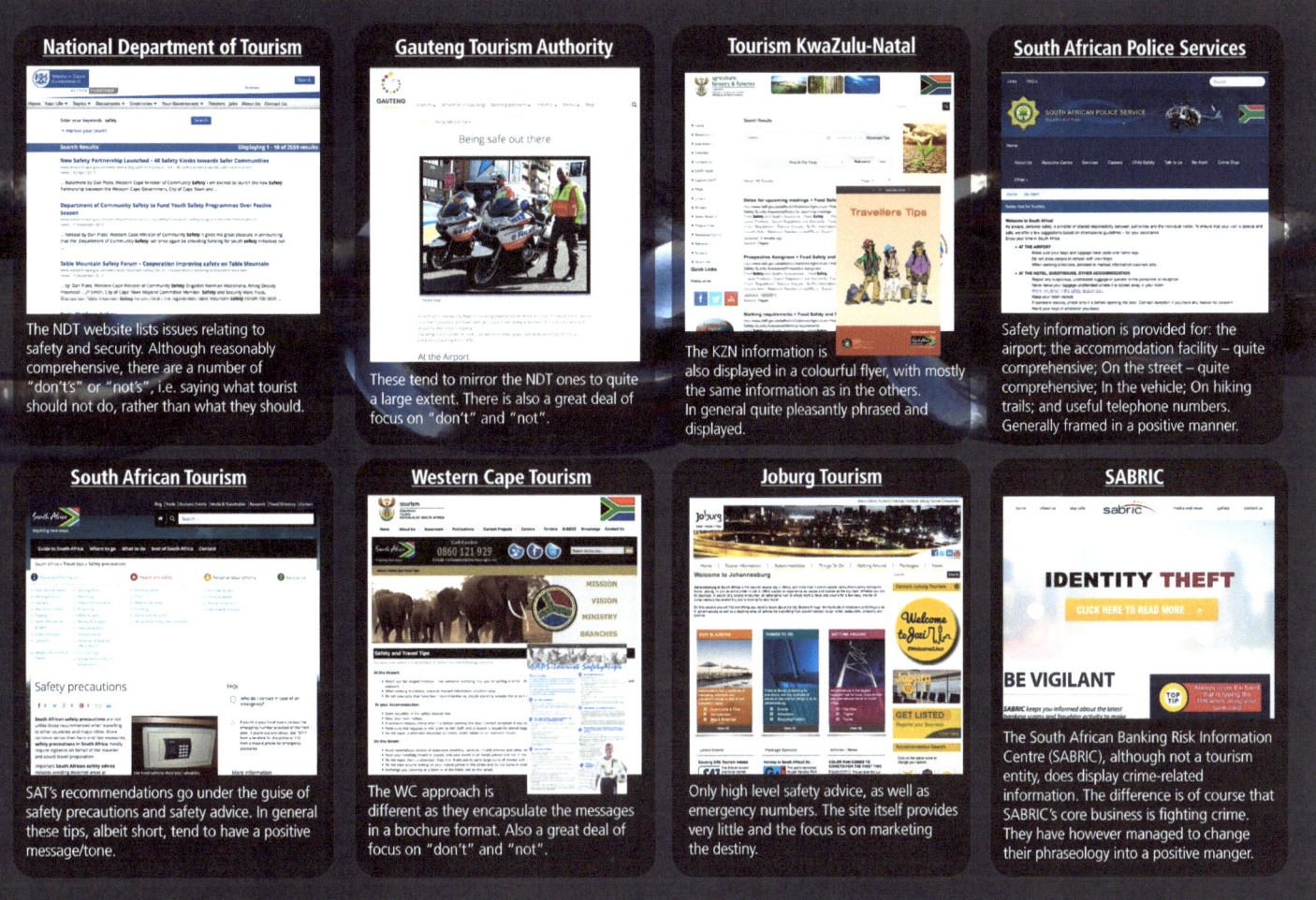

National Department of Tourism

The NDT website lists issues relating to safety and security. Although reasonably comprehensive, there are a number of "don't's" or "not's", i.e. saying what tourist should not do, rather than what they should.

Gauteng Tourism Authority

At the Airport

These tend to mirror the NDT ones to quite a large extent. There is also a great deal of focus on "don't" and "not".

Tourism KwaZulu-Natal

The KZN information is also displayed in a colourful flyer, with mostly the same information as in the others. In general quite pleasantly phrased and displayed.

South African Police Services

Safety information is provided for: the airport; the accommodation facility – quite comprehensive; On the street – quite comprehensive; In the vehicle; On hiking trails; and useful telephone numbers. Generally framed in a positive manner.

South African Tourism

SAT's recommendations go under the guise of safety precautions and safety advice. In general these tips, albeit short, tend to have a positive message/tone.

Western Cape Tourism

The WC approach is different as they encapsulate the messages in a brochure format. Also a great deal of focus on "don't" and "not".

Joburg Tourism

Only high level safety advice, as well as emergency numbers. The site itself provides very little and the focus is on marketing the destiny.

SABRIC

The South African Banking Risk Information Centre (SABRIC), although not a tourism entity, does display crime-related information. The difference is of course that SABRIC's core business is fighting crime. They have however managed to change their phraseology into a positive manger.

---

is a joint, integrated strategy on how to handle the communication of safety and security messages horizontally and vertically throughout the tourism spectrum in a fused public and private sector approach".

On the issue of providing safety and security information, the business tourism sector fares no better than its leisure tourism counterparts.

A search for the terms 'safety' and 'security' on the South African National Convention Bureau website delivers zero results. This despite the fact that the country has an excellent track record for hosting international events, and has hence gained experience in managing safety and security issues.

Responding to a travel safety alert issued by the US Embassy in Pretoria on 04 June 2016 (relating to 'Threats to Shopping Areas and Malls'), Tourism Minister Derek Hanekom issued a press release to reassure travellers to South Africa of their safety, by saying:

"The alerts issued periodically by other governments to their citizens around the world as a standard precautionary measure have been noted. We can understand that alerts of this nature may cause anxiety and fear amongst some travellers and members of the trade who want to advise their clients responsibly. Tourists to South Africa should be aware that our security services are working with their counterparts in countries around the world on these concerns, and are liaising closely with our business community to secure the safety of our citizens and visitors."

I am astounded that Minister Hanekom did not take the opportunity in his statement to refer readers to the TSI website, which has a reasonably comprehensive list of 'Traveller's Tips' advice.

Being a private sector initiative, the TSI is partly funded by the TBCSA through funds generated by the TOMSA tourism levy, which the TBCSA administers. Why then has the TSI not been tasked by the TBCSA to deliver the 'integrated strategy on how to handle the communication of safety and security messages' goals as outlined by van Vuuren? I originally published van Vuuren's article 'Tourism Security: A Comparison on Safety Tips' in May 2016 and re-published the article again in January 2017.

Come to think of it, why has South African Tourism not taken the lead by creating a 'safety & security' page on the 'travel trade partners' website that links to the TSI website? I even checked the 'related sites' section of the trade website and see no mention of the TSI at all. In fact there's no mention of, or link to, the TSI on the TOMSA website either. Doesn't say much for industry collaboration!

I'm sure that many private sector inbound tourism marketing websites, who collectively reach out to millions of potential visitors, would be happy to create a link to the TSI website for safety and security advice, if the information is as positive and concise as van Vuuren alludes to.

In conclusion, for South Africa to compete on the global tourism stage as a safe destination, it is imperative that safety and security issues are communicated to prospective tourists and event planners in a positive and proactive manner. And that both the public and private sectors of the South African tourism industry collaborate to get the job done. 🅣

The role of
TOUR OPERATORS
in
SAFARI BOOKINGS

Research suggests that travellers are changing their booking habits by making reservations directly on booking aggregators or directly via the safari lodge or game reserve's website. So where does this trend leave Tour Operators? Is the traditional travel distribution channel changing from a three-tier level (Customer – Travel Agent – Tour Operator - Supplier) to a one-level (Customer - Supplier) approach?

By **Des Langkilde**.

According to McKinsey & Company, *'Suppliers are making huge investments to lure customers to their direct channels, inadvertently reducing the return on investment (ROI) by lifting costs with little immediate increase in revenue. Online aggregators are not only pushing suppliers out and undermining their one-stop-shop proposition but also digging their heels into a format that emphasises price as the primary product differentiator'*. McKinsey suggests that *'Suppliers should shift from a business-to-business, channel-centric approach to a decidedly customer-centric one: the overarching goal [being] to win customers, not to fight a zero-sum game with intermediaries.'*

Looking for answers to substantiate McKinsey's observation, and to establish the role of Tour Operators as a source for safari bookings specifically, I turned to Vernon Wait, Marketing Director of Lalibela Private Game Reserve in South Africa's malaria-free Eastern Cape province.

"Itineraries to Africa can be complicated and require specialised knowledge. Things can go wrong in Africa and that is when a client needs to be able to go to their travel professional for assistance as opposed to a 'call centre in the Philippines' for those who may have booked via other channels," says Wait.

"While we do not ignore the direct market, tour operators and travel agents remain the single largest source of business to Lalibela and we see no reason why this should not remain so for the foreseeable future.

"This business is all about relationships. A safari property like Lalibela, who thinks long term, would never discard the travel trade simply because, for example, the industry is going through a boom period now and the direct channel might be more lucrative and appealing.

"Lalibela, now under new ownership, is making huge investments in purchasing and rehabilitating additional land, upgrading lodges and WiFi connectivity, and adding more game. We believe very strongly that it is in our interest to build up strong relationships with the trade in the belief that we are there to support each other, through good times and through more challenging times. We will continue to build on existing relationships and to forge new relationships going forward," Wait concludes.

So, it's really about relationships, which is where online aggregators lose out. They may provide quick price comparisons but unknown to most travellers, booking through a tour operator can, in fact, cost less, especially when an extended tour itinerary is required.

Tour operators pre-negotiate the best prices and have done the necessary due diligence needed to find the traveller the best deal to suit his or her pocket. Tour operators also have access to specials, exclusive deals, and upgrades, and add the personal touch that is not available through online booking aggregators.

Another important benefit to booking through a tour operator is when there are unforeseen changes that arise before or during a trip. Tour operators have better access to resources and can quickly handle flight delays and change schedules, accommodation reservations, visa issues, and the like without necessarily demanding additional fees.

Consumers more often than not, don't realise the personalised service offered by tour operators until such time as they need it. Tour operators are available before, during and after the trip, they are on hand 24/7 to provide assistance. This is not always the case when trying to contact your online supplier! On top of which there is no one else to blame

if elements of the travel itinerary are disappointing – there is no agency to blame or help to solve problems.

Conclusion

For consumers, booking aggregators have made it easier to research and compare travel destination product prices. It's a fact that every year the number and proportion of aggregator and OTA bookings rise. Whilst there are perhaps compelling reasons to book a city break in a first world country online, there are many more factors at play when booking a trip to Africa, so travellers need to consider their motivations carefully.

It's also a fact that credible tour operators add value to the price proposition by providing buyer reassurance and added value through, for example, financial guarantees. The Southern Africa Tourism Services Association (SATSA) bonding scheme is a good example, whereby deposits held by the tour operator are refunded to the client (or the tour passed to another member to fulfil) in the event of the member's involuntary liquidation. 🆃

Definitions:

Booking Aggregator: *An aggregator refers to a web site* [or meta-search engine] *that aggregates specific information from multiple online sources. Aggregators troll the results of booking engines and return the best results* [including the hotel's own website, which often offers specials and deals that the OTA's can't match]. Research suggests that while most travellers are still conducting their primary research on an aggregator site, they are increasingly turning to the brand itself once they're prepared to book.

Online Travel Agent: *An online travel agent (OTA) allows travellers to book* [flights, holiday packages, hotel rooms, car rentals, train tickets, etc] *from a single website*. It's interesting to note that Lalibela Private Game Reserve achieved a rating of 9.5 (out of 10) in the booking.com Guest Review Awards for 2016.

Market Intelligence Report

SATSA — Southern Africa Tourism Services Association

 Grant Thornton

The information below was extracted from data available as at **09 February 2017**. By **Martin Jansen van Vuuren** of **Grant Thornton**.

ARRIVALS

The latest available data from **Statistics South Africa** is for **January** to **November 2016***:

	Current period	Change over same period last year
UK	394 378	11.8%
Germany	280 229	22.2%
USA	313 704	16.8%
India	88 796	23.3%
China (incl Hong Kong)	109 698	42.7%
Overseas Arrivals	2 271 322	18.9%
African Arrivals	6 771 036	11.6%
Total Foreign Arrivals	9 079 056	13.3%

HOTEL STATS

The latest available data from **STR Global** is for **January** to **November 2016**:

Current period	Average Room Occupancy (ARO)	Average Room Rate (ARR)	Revenue Per Available Room (RevPAR)
All Hotels in SA	65.3%	R 1 164	R 759
All 5-star hotels in SA	66.0%	R 2 133	R 1 407
All 4-star hotels in SA	65.1%	R 1 078	R 701
All 3-star hotels in SA	65.5%	R 916	R 601
Change over same period last year			
All Hotels in SA	2.7%	8.9%	11.9%
All 5-star hotels in SA	4.7%	10.9%	16.1%
All 4-star hotels in SA	3.4%	6.7%	10.4%
All 3-star hotels in SA	3.2%	6.1%	9.5%

ACSA DATA

The latest available data from **ACSA** is for **January** to **December 2016**:

Change over same period last year	Passengers arriving on International Flights	Passengers arriving on Regional Flights	Passengers arriving on Domestic Flights
OR Tambo International	3.0%	3.4%	4.5%
Cape Town International	15.7%	18.6%	5.4%
King Shaka International	20.1%	N/A	7.4%

CAR RENTAL DATA

The latest available data from **SAVRALA** is for **January** to **May 2016**:

	Current period	Change over same period last year
Industry Rentals	1 134 620	-1%
Industry Utilisation	74.2%	3.6%
Industry Revenue	2 375 892 450	10%

WHAT THIS MEANS FOR MY BUSINESS

The data continues to indicate recovery of both the foreign leisure and domestic business market. The outlook for 2017 is cautiously optimistic. The settling of the effects of events such as Brexit and the USA elections, coupled to the improvement in economic growth in South Africa's main foreign source markets should aid growth in foreign tourism to South Africa. South African politics and slow economic recovery will dampen growth in the domestic leisure and business markets. It should be borne in mind that tourism growth in 2016 was on top of a dismal 2015, and although growth in tourism is expected, the high growth rates experienced in 2016 is unlikely to be repeated in 2017.

*Note that African Arrivals plus Overseas Arrivals do not add to Total Foreign Arrivals due to the exclusion of unspecified arrivals, which could not be allocated to either African or Overseas.

For more information contact Martin at Grant Thornton on +27 (0)21 417 8838 or visit: http://www.gt.co.za

TOURISM BUSINESS INDEX

Mainstreaming Travel and Tourism in the South African Economy

TRAVEL AND TOURISM BUSINESS PERFORMANCE RISES IN Q4 2016

By **Kagiso Mosue**.

Outlook for Q1 2017

Anticipated business performance for Q1 2017 is moderately low at an index of 96.0, reflecting a slightly depressed outlook. Performance for the Accommodation segment is expected to remain fairly flat, whilst the 'Other Tourism Business' segment looks forward to a continued positive run.

Looking ahead to the rest of the year, the industry looks forward to a less turbulent year. "There is no doubt that the major political and socio-economic developments that we saw unfold in 2016 will spill over to 2017. However, the TBCSA remains cautiously optimistic that travel and tourism will roll with the punches and that overall improvement in business performance will rise even further in the coming months," says Mmatšatši Ramawela, CEO of the Tourism Business Council of South Africa (TBCSA).

Image courtesy of South African Tourism

Despite the tough operating environment, the South African travel and tourism industry experienced slightly better than normal business performance in the last quarter of 2016.

Against a normal performance score of 100, the industry recorded an index of 104,5 - slightly higher than the anticipated index of 81.7.

Although performance in this quarter was the best for 2016, overall 2016 performance was slightly below 2015, and continues the soft decline seen since the best years of 2013 when the average for the year was just below 110 – once again drawing attention to the challenges businesses are facing in the operating environment.

Specific business segment performance

In Q4 2016, the 'Other Tourism Businesses' segment (comprising of tour operators, coach operators, vehicle rental companies, airlines, travel agents, retail outlets, forex traders, conference venues and attractions) recorded better than normal performance with an index score of 116.1. This is significantly higher than the forecast score of 69.9. Meanwhile, the Accommodation segment performance was below normal levels with an index of 89.5 – a score that was notably also below the expected 109.4.

Contributing Factors

The cost of inputs once again featured prominently as the greatest negative contributing factor to performance (49% for Accommodation and 41% for Other Tourism Businesses), and it has remained one for the main negative contributing factors to business performance throughout 2016.

On the positive side, strong overseas leisure demand was cited in the Accommodation index as a positive contributing factor, but this was not significant enough to lift up the overall performance for both Accommodation and 'Other Tourism Businesses' segments.

Read More:

Download the TBI Q4 Executive Summary
Download the Full TBI Q4 2016 Report

About the author: Kagiso Mosue is the Corporate Communications Manager at the Tourism Business Council of South Africa (TBCSA). www.tbcsa.travel

This information is designed to assist individual businesses, policy-makers, investors and all other relevant stakeholders, understand the travel and tourism operating environment. Th aim is to assist businesses to plan for the likely, future tourism environment. The TBI report is compiled on behalf of the TBCSA by Grant Thornton.

Recording Wildlife Spotting Online

WildSpots.org is a free iOS and Android mobile application and website for recording the migration and distribution of individual animal, bird and insect species across southern Africa. Game reserves, wildlife conservancies, NGOs and tourists alike are invited to share their wildlife sightings on this important regional database.

By **Des Langkilde**.

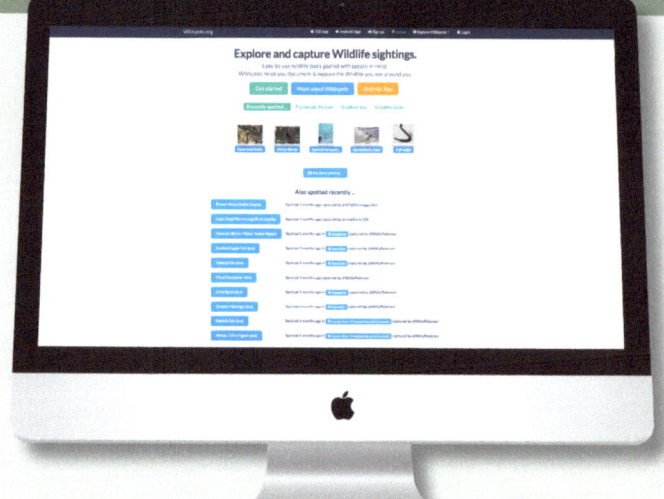

Wildspots.org was created over a decade ago when the late Wally Petersen, founder of the Kommetjie Environmental Awareness Group, started mapping the location of wildlife species on the southern Cape Peninsula. Over the years this grew into a useful database and soon interesting trends appeared on the migration and distribution of individual species.

The database was extended with Petersen's travels around southern Africa and Madagascar. In particular, studies were done on the large numbers of animals killed on the roads.

Two close friends from the eco-tourism and wildlife hospitality industries, Russ Weston and Jurie Moolman, saw the huge value in the many significant observations and in 2012 the three of them planned and developed a user-friendly recording system.

To date, WildSpots has grown to encompass over 19,026 wildlife records comprising over 1,628 unique species contributed by just 295 members. Sightings include records from Botswana, Namibia, Swaziland, Mozambique and Madagascar. Wildspots is a non-commercial, free website and the information is freely available to anyone with an interest in wildlife biodiversity. WildSpots records are contributed to the ADU and Mammal Map databases.

About the founders

The senseless murder of WildSpots founder and environmental activist Wally Petersen at his home in Kommetjie in November 2016, is a sad loss to conservation efforts in Africa.

Co-founder Jurie Moolman is a hospitality provider and owner of Djuma Game Reserve – a 9,000 ha private game reserve, which forms part of the Sabi Sands Private Nature Reserve and the Greater Kruger National Park. He is also involved in breeding rare and endangered animals at his 35, 000 ha Thaba Tholo facility near Thabazimbi.

The third co-founder of WildSpots is Russ Weston of Greenlife Africa. He is a nature ambassador and a pioneer of experiential travel in Southern Africa. Before starting Greenlife in 1992, Russ spent time as a research assistant and specialist nature guide leading expeditions throughout Southern Africa.

Since Petersen's demise, Tourism Tattler has come onboard to continue his legacy by administrating the WildSpots online assets as a service to the travel industry and is offering a special company membership badge to those members and websites that promote Wildspots to their guests. Experts are needed to assist with identification and systems to categorise the wealth of biodiversity and Tourism Tattler is appealing to the travel industry to assist in various areas.

Citizen Science

The WildSpots system provides excellent tools for specific research projects for closed and public collaboration.

Wally Petersen's original aim was to make Wildspots available to schools throughout southern Africa, particularly those in the rural areas where biodiversity information would be particularly valuable. "I believe that young wildlife observers will have a better chance of becoming young conservationists. The power of observation can never be underestimated. There is a growing global trend that recognises the value of Citizen Science" said Petersen when Tourism Tattler interviewed him in 2013.

"The tourism industry can make a huge contribution as WildSpots provides a great opportunity for tourists to make a meaningful contribution by logging species they encounter during their safari activities. By observing and recording the wildlife sightings around them, the visitor's experience will be enhanced" said Petersen.

WildSpots members can set up their own unique focus area to map and record species sightings with the greatest of ease. Guests will have a personal record of their visit with great features including wildlife checklists, location maps and field notes. Of value to property owners are the tools within Wildspots to accurately define their reserve boundaries and invite contributors and members.

WildSpots features

Record

A Record represents a wildlife sighting that has been captured on Wildspots.org – at its most basic, it includes uploaded images of the species of wildlife spotted, along with the date and the geographical position, assisted with Google Maps. In addition, the Record can include a specific time and field notes.

Start recording your wildlife sightings and let your rangers and guests document their encounters on unique personal and collaborative maps.

MobiApp

The free Mobile Application makes it easy to upload wildlife sightings from Android smartphones or tablet devices while out of Internet and cellphone range. The MobiApp will store the user's records and publish them to wildspots.org when back within WiFi or signal range. These basic records are available for editing, verification and adding field notes and images at a later stage.

To date Wildspots contributors have recorded over 1,628 wildlife species, which include:

- 11,196 Birds (813 species)
- 4,906 Mammals (181 species)
- 1,734 Reptiles (242 species)
- 745 Amphibians (92 species)
- 232 Insects (184 species)
- 207 Others (116 species).

Timeline Map

Users can explore wildlife records on a map and adjust the time range of when these records were seen. The map can also be adjusted to only show species of particular interest.

The free WildSpots mobile application for iOS and Android makes recording wildlife sightings easy even when out of WiFi range.

Records

The most recent of all wildlife records can be filtered by species (Mammal, Reptile, Bird, etc), with or without a photo as well as adjust the time range.

Photos

Species identification is enhanced through a Wikipedia link for information and photos of animals. In addition, an AnimalWiki database of animal species that contains basic information, such as common and scientific names, distribution maps and photos, is integrated into the website.

Groups

Allows users with a shared wildlife interest to form a Group and contribute records to the Group - much like a Facebook or LinkedIn Group.

WildSpots users can easily create their own Group or join an existing Group that focuses on a specific geographic area, wildlife category or species. All members have access to collaborative records, which can be marked as private or shared.

Add your Game Reserve

Wildspots Areas allows users to explore areas around southern Africa and get an insight about what wildlife is being spotted there. This tool builds dynamic checklists for the area. The data can also be downloaded in an Excel file format.

Game and nature reserves are welcome to use WildSpots as an added value tool for their visitors and guest to record their wildlife sightings while visiting the property.

Wildspots For You

Let's all collaborate and enjoy sharing Africas' wildlife heritage.

Wildspots is a free service for your unlimited use. Assist in creating an audit of southern Africa's wildlife heritage, noting the existence of species and affording them the recognition and protection that they deserve.

Sponsors and partners are invited to assist in growing this legacy initiative in memory of Wally Petersen, who devoted so much time to his passion for wildlife conservation.

For more information call +27 (0)82 374 7260 or email wildspotsorg@gmail.com or visit www.wildspots.org

The image below of a Water Monitor (Varanus niloticus) sighting on the author's eco estate property in Ballito, KwaZulu-Natal was loaded onto the Wildspots website. It just goes to show that even amateurs can contribute to the database.

The A-B-C's of RÉUNION ISLAND

Réunion Island is a mere 4-hour flight from Johannesburg on Air Austral and South African passport holders do not require visas for this tropical paradise which makes it the perfect destination!

Located in the Indian Ocean, east of Madagascar and 175 kilometres south-west of Mauritius, it is a region of France and is known for its volcanic, rain-forested interior, offshore reefs, beaches and Creole culture. Here are some facts about this gorgeous island as well as what to do and see:

Flights & Accommodation

Air Austral offers direct flights to Réunion Island between Johannesburg and Réunion Island three times a week.

Visit *www.AirAustral.com* for flight details and browse a range of accommodation options on the official tourism site at *en.reunion.fr*

Reunion Island

Geography and Climate

Erosion and volcanic activity have left Réunion Island's landscape uneven yet a paradise to be explored.

Nature

Réunion boasts a varied plant life and a diverse flora and more than a third of Réunion's surface is still covered with forests and wild plants.

Adventure on the Island

The Réunion Island is beaming with adventures waiting to be discovered. Hiking trails, diving, helicopter flights and paragliding, there is no end to the activity list that is yours on your arrival. Jet Skiing, Kite surfing, or some good paddling is yet another way in which Réunion promises to thrill adventure seekers. Big game fishing, sailing or simply swimming in the ocean makes sure that there is something for every visitor.

Food

Gastronomical pleasures are of great importance on the island, and the Réunionese have a wide range of culinary traditions which they love to cook. Take French culture as a base, add a pinch of Malagasy customs, a zest of Chinese know-how, a bit of Indian savour, and you'll get a unique exotic recipe.

Meet New Cultures

A visit to this Indian Ocean paradise, Réunion Island, allows travellers to discover a history shaped by people from Africa, Madagascar, Europe and Asia. The universal challenge of racial and ethnic mixing is dispelled on Réunion Island as its people warmly demonstrate how things should and can be done.

Travel Tips

- South African passport holders do not require a visa.

- The currency used on Réunion Island is the euro (€).

- French is the official language of Réunion Island, but communicating in English is possible.

- The average annual temperature on Réunion Island is 24 degrees Celsius.

- There is no malaria, and no travel vaccines are required.

- Réunion Island time is two hours ahead of South Africa.

- All plug points on Réunion Island are two-point – take adaptors with you.

REUNION ISLAND

THE ULTIMATE EXPERIENCE

Réunion Island Tourism Board is represented by Atout France in South Africa.

CONTACTS:

 +27 (0)11 010 205 0201

 reunionisland.za@atout-france.fr

 GotoReunionSA

 @reuniontourisme

 @reuniontourisme

 blog.welcometoreunionisland.com

Exploring
SRI LANKA
from Tangalle to Galle

Sri Lanka (formerly Ceylon) – an island south of India – is renown for its diverse landscape, ranging from rainforest and arid plains to highlands and sandy beaches. In this review we explore the coastal hotels from Tangalle to Galle.

▲ *Amanwella Hotel beach*

By **Adam Jacot de Boinod.**

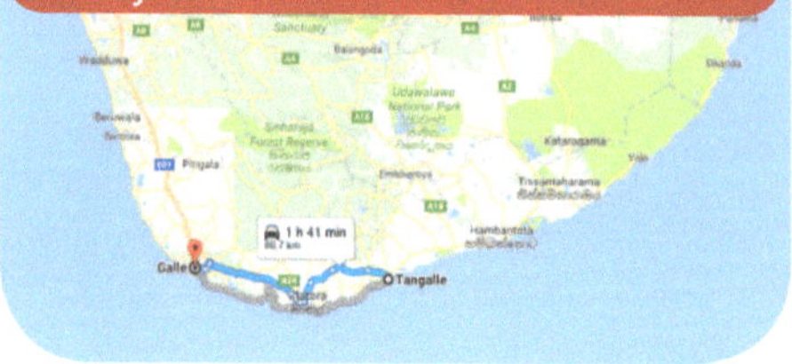

Twenty minutes after having landed, I reached my first hotel. Wallawwa is the original home of a Sinhalese family, 250 years old and now nine years into its renovated self. It's a lovely legacy of colonialism.

As I continued across the inland I got to recognise the pattern of jungle encroaching on villages that then spilt out onto streets. The neon shop signs of the towns were already familiar to me from other Asian visits, as were the locals as they went about their lives, sometimes a whole family to a bicycle.

I felt a real delight in witnessing the source of my food as manual workers, up to their knees in mud in the paddy fields, left behind them immaculate rows of rice. And to taste their rice that evening made me appreciate my food all the more.

Continuing south onto Tangalle, the home of the new Anantara resort is equipped with three great restaurants. 'Journeys' has a wide mix via a fully-stocked buffet, 'Verele' sticks to the unique flavours of Sri Lankan cooking and there's Italian food at 'Il Mare' on a cliff top overlooking the ocean. The décor is consistent with the hotel's wheel motif echoed throughout.

The next morning I walked next door to the stunning hotel Amanwella. Each room is identical in layout and design and comes with a plunge pool. The colours are harmonious and there is a zen ambience. Inside, the terrazzo flooring is in muted, sandy tones to reflect the nearby beach. The large timber sliding panels separate the interior from the exterior. Mercifully there are no televisions in the rooms.

The writer Leonard Woolf described Tangalle with great precision: *"The evening air is warm and gentle. An enormous sky meets an enormous sea. The stars blaze in the sky and blaze in the sea … there is no sound in this melodrama of a tropical night except a faint lapping of the sea, and now and then a shivery stir of palm leaves"*. And it's true – at Amanwella there is a real paradise. The golden beach, curving for half a mile in a gentle arc, is flanked by two rocky headlands. The water is crystal clear and the sand is fine and powdery.

I then headed inland to Lake Koggolo and onto my next hotel, the Kahanda Kanda with all the trappings of colonial life so reassuringly familiar to Brits. From my breakfast table, I could just about make out Koggolo Lake. I decided to take a boat trip and visit the Buddhist monastery.

▼ *Wallawwa Main Hotel*   ▼ *Anantara Peace Haven Hotel Ile Mare*   ▼ *Kahanda Kanda Hotel Pool*

INDIA

SRI LANKA

QUICK FACTS

Sri Lanka is famed for its ancient Buddhist ruins, including the 5th-century citadel Sigiriya, with its palace and frescoes. Sri Lanka has many ruins dating back more than 2,000 years.

Capitals: Sri Jayawardenepura Kotte, Colombo | **Population**: 20.48 million (2013).
National anthem: Sri Lanka Matha | **Official languages**: Sinhala, Tamil, English.

▲ *Amangalla Hotel*

Maliga Kandy was my next hotel. It's part of the Hideaways Club Classic Collection portfolio – ideal for someone who doesn't want to be restricted to one location. Malinga Kandy a gem in the jungle, built in 2010, it offers something for everyone with seven bedrooms including a separate cottage for teenagers. The staff, comprised of security, cooks, cleaners and gardeners, are attentive and charming.

The lovely crescent beach at Unawatuna has beautiful yellow sand but suffers from over-tourism. I managed to regain a sense of peace at the nearby Japanese pagoda with its pure white paint offset on all four sides by gold statues. It has an impressive 360-degree view of the jungle, the bay and the Galle fort I was soon to visit. I had a sense of innocence at the local railway station that is a wonderful throwback in time with old-fashioned timetables behind glass frames and I would love to have had time to be a passenger snaking through all that wonderful landscape.

Then on to Amangalla. While clearly the supreme standard of an Aman hotel, it must have been given quite a makeover. The 'Zaal' (hall) has white walls with angled mirrors that reflect the light and the candles, and it's furnished with rattan chairs and sofas. The high ceiling has overhead fans and modern metallic chandeliers.

In 1850 there used to be a 45-minute pigeon post from Galle to Colombo, flying at some 85mph, established by The Observer newspaper. Even with the new motorway, it was bound to take me a little longer to reach the capital. Transport has its own challenges with the right of way always open to question. So renting a car would not be my suggestion. Tuk-tuks are fun, especially on the minor roads. While dishing out advice, I stress you just have to respect the midday intensity of the sun and likewise the savage currents of the Indian Ocean.

And onto to my final destination – Maniumpathy. The eight suites with artefacts and vintage furnishings are named after the members of a fifth generation Tamil family from Jaffna (where Manipay was a thriving and wealthy locality). It worked perfectly for me as a base for Colombo before my final journey home.

Ayubowan! (The Sinhalese word for every form of greeting stretching from 'good morning', 'good afternoon', 'good evening', 'good night' to 'good-bye').

About the author: *Tourism Tattler correspondent,* **Adam Jacot de Boinod** *is the author of 'The Meaning of Tingo and Other Extraordinary Words from around the World', published by Penguin Books. While researching this article, Adam travelled with support from The Holiday Place (www.holidayplace.co.uk).*

▼ *Malinga Kandy Hotel Gazebo*   ▼ *Amangalla Hotel*   ▼ *Maniumpathy Hotel*

Tourism Tattler has joined the Global Travel Blogger & Social Media Influencer Summit as a media partner, which takes place in India from 26 - 28 September 2017.

Bloggers and influencers have emerged as the key channels of marketing for tourism across the world. Most travellers rely on information and opinions of digital media when making travel purchase decisions. While some tourism boards and travel companies have realised this, most are still trying to figure how to use this force to their advantage.

Hence the significance of an event like BLOG IT – a global gathering of travel bloggers, influencers and media, who will come together to interact with tourism boards, companies, industry associations and Governments. The event will allow for networking and the exchange of ideas on how these stakeholders can work together for mutual benefit and the growth of global tourism.

EVENT COMPONENTS

BLOG IT will feature the following key components:
- **Conference**: Featuring a series of keynote speakers, fireside chats and panels covering a vast array of topics.
- **Storytelling**: By travellers who inspire.
- **Networking**: And Speed Dating between media and attending delegates.
- **Workshops**: Covering social media, digital marketing and PR.
- **Focus**: Tourism Board presentations about their destinations.
- **Expo**: For companies and tourism boards to display their services.
- **FAM Tours**: Across India for bloggers, media, influencers and trade delegates.

WHO SHOULD ATTEND BLOG IT?
- **Travel bloggers and influencers**: Explore a destination you may have wanted to but could not. Meet a whole new crop of brands and sponsors.
- **Tour operators, hotels and other travel businesses**: India is one of the biggest and fastest-growing markets in the world. No one can afford to stay away from it – both for inbound and outbound tourism. An ideal opportunity to build business alliances and connect with the best international travel media.

- **Tourism Boards**: This is an ideal opportunity to interact with a curated set of media from across the world for targeted messages, and to promote your destination to travel businesses.
- **Industry Associations**: To promote their members.
- **Communication Businesses and Consultants**: Understand how influencers are driving marketing and how these to benefit clients.
- **Allied sectors**: Financial institutions, insurance, technology, etc, who want to leverage influencers for their brand promotions to the travel trade and community.

VENUE

The host city will be finalised as soon as negotiations are concluded with state tourism boards. The current shortlist includes Bangalore, Khajuraho and New Delhi.

PARTNERS

BLOG IT is in talks with various organisations to come on board as partners. The Adventure Tour Operators Association of India (ATOAI) has already confirmed the same.

Off the record: Talks are on with PATA, IGLTA, ATTA, WTM and other partners who have already expressed keen interest.

ORGANISERS

The event has been curated by Ajay Jain, India's leading travel blogger, author and photographer. His publishing and events company Kunzum is putting the show together. 🇹

FOR MORE INFORMATION CONTACT

Web: *www.blogit.travel*
Email: *wetravel@kunzum.com*
Mobile: +91.9910044476
Skype: ajayjain9

Middle East's Successful 'The Hotel Show' Brand Launches in Africa

The Hotel Show Africa 2017, taking place at Gallagher Convenyion Centre, Johannesburg from 25-27 June 2017, aims to boost the African hospitality market that already has more than 350 new hotel projects in development.

dmg events - Middle East, Asia & Africa, a leading international exhibitions company, is set to launch its successful hospitality event brand in Africa. The Hotel Show Africa 2017 is the first geo-adapted event from the dmg hospitality portfolio to launch in Africa. The launch coincides with a surge in tourist numbers across the continent that is expected to attract 85 million people a year by 2020.

The new event is adapted for the African market and based on the company's highly successful The Hotel Show Dubai. It will bring together national and international exhibitors to showcase hospitality products for restaurants, cafes, bars and hotels, right through to food & beverage service outlets.

The Hotel Show Africa 2017 will focus on new trends in the hospitality sector, covering everything from technology to kitchen equipment, cleaning services to interior design, and furnishings to tableware. The event will also introduce the successful Vision Conference, a vibrant knowledge platform set to attract hundreds of senior industry leaders to discuss trends, debate challenges and spotlight opportunities in the African hospitality sector.

"Africa offers huge opportunities for hospitality providers on a continent forecast to enjoy some of the highest economic growth rates in the world," said Christine Davidson, Vice President, dmg ems Africa.

"The Hotel Show Africa 2017 is a direct recognition of the sector's growth. South Africa is the right place for this show, offering a gateway to the African market, in a country that is undergoing a strong hospitality boom with millions of dollars' investment and a government-backed recognition of the economic benefits from tourism." Davidson added.

The potential of the sector is reflected in the strategy of hotel groups already making significant investments, with 365 hotel projects in the continent's pipeline.

The Hotel Show Africa 2017 Partners

A strategic partnership with the Federated Hospitality Association of Southern Africa (FEDHASA) has already been concluded ahead of the Africa launch.

"A forum such as this brings a wealth of opportunity for owners, managers and suppliers in terms of connecting with each other, meeting new contacts, generating business but also for gaining essential insight and knowledge share, and FEDHASA is pleased to be a part of it," says Tshifhiwa Tshivhengwa, CEO of FEDHASA.

Another strategic partner is the Restaurant Association of South Africa (RASA), while the Guest House Accommodation of South Africa association (GHASA) and the Southern Africa Tourism Services Association (SATSA) have pledged their support.

As the official tourism and hospitality journal for Africa, Tourism Tattler has also come on board as a media partner to cover the Hotel Show Africa 2017 event.

Call for Vision Conference speakers

Senior professionals with something important to share are invited to submit a session topic or presentation. Submissions should be no more than 100 words, outlining the topic and why it matters, emailed to info@thehotelshowafrica.com. Or call Sean Osterloh on +27 11 783 7250 for an informal chat about the conference.

Exhibit at The Hotel Show Africa 2017

For enquiries to exhibit complete the short form at www.thehotelshowafrica.com/enquire-about-exhibiting

Register to attend

Registration to attend The Hotel Show Africa 2017 is now open at www.thehotelshowafrica.com/enquire-about-visiting

Tips on how to
DE-STRESS

The importance of making time for yourself throughout the year cannot be over emphasised. In this article, Diabetes South Africa looks at ways to de-stress your life.

By **Romy Toussaint**.

The first thing that comes to mind when you think of de-stressing is usually the thought of going away on holiday – maybe sitting on the beach or soaking up the scenery at a game reserve, but, mostly, it's waiting for your annual leave.

But is that enough? Racing through the year to get your annual leave – allowing your days to be wished away, while your personal needs and your health are neglected or put on 'hold'. But then, your leave arrives and so does that holiday and before you know it, it's over! Did you get to relax? How many days into the holiday did it take to actually relax?

The truth is you shouldn't only relax while on holiday, you should be finding ways to slow down regularly throughout the year. Relaxing equates to giving yourself time – time to put your feet up, time to unwind, time to de-stress and time to be in the moment. So, when you do have that well-deserved break at the end of the year, or whenever you can take it, it will be a wanted holiday, not a needed one! You'll arrive less stressed, and you won't have the pressure of having to de-stress and you can just enjoy it.

You may ask how do you give yourself this 'time' throughout the year? Firstly, you need to find your stress trigger – what is it that stresses you out the most? What area is the toughest for you? What is your common stress denominator?

You might not be able to change what stresses you out, but you can change how it affects you – you can change the time you give it, take control of what you can and be aware of not giving too much time to what you can't control. Then you need to figure out what activity de-stresses you the most, and when you do find it make it a priority!

Margot McCumisky, DSA's national manager, suggests five inexpensive activities to help you de-stress and unwind.

Go for a foot massage or get your children to give you a foot massage as a present.

Lounge poolside.

Enjoy a bubble bath with scented candles and a glass of wine.

Take part in a Pilates class.

"The truth is you shouldn't only relax while on holiday, you should be finding ways to slow down regularly throughout the year… So, when you do have that well-deserved break at the end of the year, or whenever you can take it, it will be a wanted holiday, not a needed one!"

Get your kids or hubby to make supper one night or a few nights.

About the author: Romy Toussaint is a teacher, trainer, mentor, coach and entrepreneur. She has specialised in the sporting industry for over 20 years and is a qualified NLP practitioner and life coach, and a T3 certified Apple trainer.

Promoting diabetes care and support for all

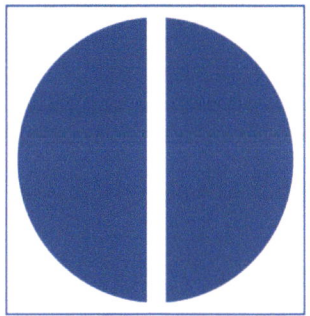

Diabetes® South Africa

Diabetes South Africa is a non-profit organisation, public benefit organisation, founded in 1969 to be a support and an advocate for all people with diabetes in South Africa.

Our Vision: The Association is committed to reducing the impact of diabetes through support, education and information.

Our Mission Statement:
Empowering all those affected by Diabetes through support, education and information.
Providing awareness to all and highlighting risk factors associated with diabetes and promoting healthy lifestyles.

Diabetes SA is primarily a volunteer organisation and relies heavily on people with diabetes and their families who pool their talents, share their knowledge and experiences and give of their time to help each other. You too could be a great organizer and get everyone off on a big walk or you may, equally valuable, be a friendly face at the end of a hospital bed.

CONTACT OUR NATIONAL OFFICE

Tel: 086 111 3913   Fax Number: 086 600 7425   Email: national@diabetessa.org.za
Visit our website for contact details of the nearest Diabetes SA branch and see where you may be able to assist others with diabetes.

www.diabetessa.org.za

Diabetes Focus eMag is the quarterly eMag of Diabetes SA and its aim is to inform, encourage and motivate people to lead a long and healthy life.

Our mission is to educate and empower people with diabetes to cope and change lifestyle habits.
Read it online at www.diabetessa.org.za

PROPERTY PROFILE

SELBORNE
GOLF ESTATE, HOTEL & SPA

R28 Million Restoration
A Success Story in The Making

After acquiring and investing R28 million into the refurbishment of the Selborne Golf Estate, Hotel and Spa, new owners, First Hotels, is seeing the benefits of an eight-figure investment that has laid a solid foundation for this well-earned 4-star gem to soar on South Africa's KwaZulu-Natal south coast.

Following extensive renovations that required the full closure of the Hotel, Selborne proudly re-opened its doors to showcase its grand makeover, which has also had a positive 'ripple effect' for the golf estate with a record-breaking 15 properties sold since the refurbishment after a 5-year period of dormant sales.

"This bears testament to a renewed investor confidence under the new management banner of the First Hotels brand, and we are extremely proud to be the catalyst to the rejuvenation of the country's first residential golf estate. Rarely do you have the opportunity to restore the grandeur of a Hotel so rich in heritage and to breathe new life into period architecture that dates back to the mid 1900's," said Tim Spencer, First Hotels Operations Director.

This was achieved by preserving the original features, such as the fine oak panelling, window panes and flooring that was originally imported

▼ The luxury Presidential Suite

▼ Hunters lounge at the Selborne

▼ Fine dining

QUICK LINKS

Old Main Road, Pennington, KwaZulu-Natal, South Africa.

+27 (0)39 688 1800

sbreservations@firstresorts.co.za

www.selbornehotel.com

GDS CODES

Amadeus: DURSEL
Galileo: C0456
Sabre: 305805
Worldspan: DURSH

The signature oak stairway, which is a main feature of the Selborne Hotel Reception

from England. "The appeal of this distinguished hotel is that we are now able to offer our guests a sentiment of yesteryear, which sets this vacation experience in a class of its own," adds Spencer.

Signature era details, like the warm oak stairway and spectacular chandeliers, have been seamlessly combined with modern luxuries. The design team's carefully handpicked selection of sleek fabrics, bespoke furnishings and a selection of fine art compliments the Hotel's heritage, striking a perfect balance between modern and period charm. The rooms, suites, bar, dining and lounge areas have been individually refurbished with the inference that it feels more like a beautiful private residence of days gone by than a traditional hotel.

The most prominent feature and prized offering is still the 18-hole championship golf course which was designed by Denis Barker, one of the original proprietors of Selborne, and is today proudly ranked in the top 100 golf destinations.

The grandiose Hotel, or also referred to as the Manor House, is complimented by a sparkling outdoor pool, lush coastal gardens, a private beach club and tennis courts. Dining options range from the relaxed atmosphere of The Terrace, to the more formal elegance of The Lord Selborne Restaurant and the convivial atmosphere of Barker's Bar or the Piano Lounge.

The world-class wellness spa is fully equipped with a sauna, express gym and four private treatment lounges. A state-of-the-art conference and banqueting facility caters for a wide array of event requirements, and the quaint wedding chapel is the perfect location for an unforgettable celebration with a grandeur of a former era.

"We are confident that the Selborne Golf Estate, Hotel and Spa is destined to become the most sought-after holiday destination and residential investment on the KwaZulu-Natal south coast," concludes Spencer.

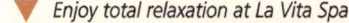
▼ *Enjoy total relaxation at La Vita Spa*

▼ *18-hole golf course*

The Old-school GENERAL MANAGER

Not the ideal Hotel General Manager. John Cleese in the epic comedy show Faulty Towers © BBC Worldwide.

There's been something fundamental missing in the last decade of hotel management: the unflashy, workaholic general managers, those who started their careers waiting tables, scrubbing kitchen counters and floors, climbing the ladder, slowly learning ALL of the necessary skills to eventually become THE General Manager.

By **Guy Stehlik**.

I grew up with the old-school generation of hospitality lads and lasses, regarding them as true hoteliers. You would find them having a drink with a guest or welcoming a tour group, having a coffee with the PCO at the breakfast session, or even better, spoiling their entire team with a sampling of the latest menu.

In the past, the reputation of South African Hotel General Managers (and chefs) was so highly celebrated that they were quickly snapped up by international hotels and hotel groups, many moving to Dubai and Europe. Albeit a testament to the quality of our training in those days, this trend of moving away created a skills drain, resulting in a new generation of General Managers who rose too quickly, skipped a few training steps, were over-promoted and found themselves at the helm of a hotel in a heartbeat as opposed to a lifetime, easily recognisable (when they emerge from behind their computer screen): young and sexy, well-dressed, flashy, living large, hotel 'bosses'.

At BON Hotels, we've decided to screen our GMs more thoroughly again. We are on a hunt-down for those old school grizzly GMs. While we do value the potential in our youth, too many shortcomings of these new-age General Managers can be attributed to quick easy promotions. I've encountered one too many young General Managers who cannot calculate their Average Daily Rate (ADR) and Revenue Per Available Room (REVPAR). Yes, I understand that there are new burdens on today's General Managers and administration demands have increased, but that should never be at the expense of an hotelier's ultimate judge – the guest.

Consider the last time you were a guest at a hotel. Did you meet the General Manager? Did you even notice him walking around?

I am reminded of wise words of one of my seniors during my training years: "If your guests are around, you should be around". Hotel management is not a 9 to 5 career, not in the least! General

Managers must be on the hotel floor during peak times: breakfast, check out, check in and dinner. An old-school hotelier wouldn't dream of clocking in at 9, filling his day with meetings, submerging himself in admin and packing up his desk at 5 to hit the gym. Surely, hotel wannabees know that they are signing up for a demanding lifestyle career?

Excellent hotel managers are those who are building amazing relationships with hotel guests, having a drink at the bar with loyal customers, making certain their staff are well cared for, and in return, their hotels are thriving. Yes, they may cost the hotel a bit more due to years of experience, but the return on investment will be worth it.

About the author: Guy Stehlik is the CEO and founder of BON Hotels. With an innate enthusiasm and dedication to the hotel industry, Guy's innovative and creative approach has ensured a successful and impressive career spanning many years as an hotelier and hotel owner.

For more info visit www.bonhotels.com/blog

MOBILE IMAGES & EMPLOYEE PRIVACY

This court case is important for Human Resource managers as it highlights the fact that although an employee has a right to privacy, it is not absolute and cannot be relied upon by an employee acting with ulterior motives to retain an employer's confidential information.

By **Fiona Leppan**.

A recent court case *(NUMSA and Another vs Rafee N.O. and Others: JR1022/12) [2016] ZALCJHB 512)*, involved the employer's instruction that the employee hand over his mobile phone for inspection. The employee refused, claiming that the employer's instruction violated his right to privacy.

The employer's instruction emanated from a report that the employee had taken photographs using his mobile phone of the company's production line, shift machines and letter trays. The employee was instructed to delete the photographs relating to the company's confidential business operations and to confirm that he had done so. When the employer asked for confirmation that the photographs had been deleted from his mobile phone, the employee replied "no comment". Thereafter, the employer instructed the employee to make his phone available to confirm that the disputed images had been removed.

The employee refused on the basis that it was his private phone that contained his personal information. The employee also argued that the employer had no right to look at his phone.

The Company asserted that its business operations needed to be kept confidential and that it operated in a competitive environment. The employee was charged and dismissed for failing to delete the images or confirming that he had done so, and for refusing to make available his mobile phone for inspection. The employee challenged the fairness of his dismissal at the CCMA, where he denied that he took the photographs.

The CCMA arbitrating commissioner found that, in the circumstances, the employer's instruction to hand over the phone was reasonable and that the employee's failure to obey the instruction warranted dismissal.

Dissatisfied with the arbitrator's outcome, the employee applied to the Labour Court to review the award. The Labour Court referred to the employee's right to maintain the confidential nature of information on his mobile phone as well as the employer's right to maintain the confidential information about its business. It held that although the employee is entitled to the privacy of the information on his mobile phone, *"that does not entitle him to use his personal phone as a camera to capture confidential information belonging to his employer in which it has a proprietary interest. When he did that, he could hardly maintain that his right to preserve the confidentiality of his personal data entitled him to retain data about the company he had obtained without permission, which was stored on the same device."* It also held that *"the action of taking such photographs is indistinguishable in principle from copying plans of the company's production layout and putting those copies in a personal briefcase."*

The Labour Court dismissed the employee's review application and held that it was not unreasonable to infer that the employee took the photographs, failed to delete them, and retained them on his mobile phone. It also held that this conduct seriously undermined the trust relationship between the employer and employee.

About the Author: Fiona Leppan is a Director in Cliffe Dekker Hofmeyr's Employment Practice.

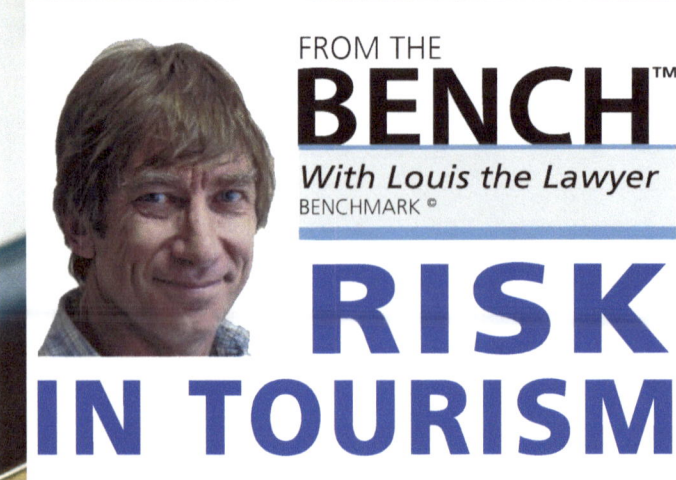

FROM THE

BENCH™

With Louis the Lawyer
BENCHMARK ©

RISK
IN TOURISM

THE LAW: CONTRACTS

- Part 26 -

The Role of:
Service Level Agreements

Alternative Dispute Resolutions (Cont'd)

As mentioned at the end of my article on standard terms and conditions last month (Part 25 - JAN 2017), I'll take a brief look at other clauses that could provide for alternative dispute resolution ('ADR') before we focus on arbitration and mediation, so here it is!

The best-known form of resolving a dispute is usually initiated by the brave words *'I'll see you in court'* or *'Speak my lawyer'*. If you choose that route, make sure that you have DEEP pockets, do not litigate on matters of principal and remember, there is no such thing as 'A WATERTIGHT CASE'! Whilst it is your democratic and constitutional right to pursue your interests in the legal forum of your choice (i.e. Small Claims Court, Labour Court, Magistrates Court, High Court, Supreme Court of Appeal or Constitutional Court), litigation should be kept in reserve for as few applications as possible and ONLY once you've exhausted ALL the alternatives. There is however no denying that in certain circumstances a summons is the correct and most effective manner in which to protect or recover your rights and interests.

One of the key benefits of ADR is the issue of privacy – the complete lack thereof was illustrated in the case of City of Cape Town v SANRAL in 2015 – prior to this case the general public (and therefore the press!) only had access to documents filed in court proceedings once the matter has been called in open court. However, the Supreme Court of Appeal ('SCA') ruled in this case that access is allowed as soon as the documents are filed/lodged and such access is allowed to *'any person'* and no *'direct legal interest'* is required. Clearly, this can have devastating consequences for your brand and that should be a key consideration: disputes are often more about brand management than about who is right or wrong!

So, now that you've made the wise decision that your welfare is more important than that of the legal fraternity, let's look at your remaining options:

We've discussed arbitration and mediation. As indicated, the latter is a form of ADR ('Alternative Dispute Resolution'). What are the others?

SUMMARY: (Click on the **MONTH / YEAR** to download the PDF)

Part 1 (page 36 **AUG 2014**), categorised risk into five sections; 1. PEOPLE, 2. MONEY, 3. LAW, 4. SERVICE and 5. ECOLOGY.

Part 2 (page 22 **SEP 2014**), covered PEOPLE under four sub-categories: Staff (discussed in Part 1); Third party service providers ('TPSP'); and Business Associates.

Part 3 (page 24 **OCT 2014**), continued with PEOPLE as Customers.

Part 4 (page 27 **NOV 2014**), started the discussion on MONEY in terms of CASH and CHEQUES.

Part 5 (page 23 **DEC 2014**), covered CREDIT and CREDIT CARDS.

Part 6 (page 25 **JAN 2015**), started the LAW category with CONTRACTS - an introduction and Requisite #1: Offer & Acceptance.

Part 7 (page 18 **FEB 2015**), continued with Requisite #1 covering telephone enquiries, e-mails, websites and advertising.

Part 8 (page 17 **MAR 2015**), covered Requisites #2: Legally Binding Obligation, and #3: Consensus in contracts.

Part 9 (page 20 **APR 2015**), covered Requisite #4: Performance Must Be Possible.

Part 10 (page 31 **MAY 2015**), covered Requisites #5: Performance Must Be Permissible, and #6: Capacity of the Contracting Parties.

Part 11 (page 21 **JUN 2015**), continued with Requisite #6: Capacity of the Contracting Parties.

Part 12 (page 23 **JUL 2015**), covered Requisite #7 Negotiating a Contract.

Part 13 (page 30 **AUG 2015**), covered Requisite #8 Drafting a Contract.

Part 14 (page 30 **OCT 2015**), covered Requisite #9 Contract Management.

Part 15 (page 26 **NOV 2015**), covered Requisite #10 Enforcing a Contract

Part 16 (page 22 **DEC 2016**), Requisite #10 Enforcing a Contract (cont'd)

Part 17 (page 23 **JAN 2016**), Requisite #10 Enforcing a Contract (cont'd)

Part 18 (page 23 **MAY 2016**), Requisite #10 Enforcing a Contract (cont'd)

Part 19 (page 24 **JUN 2016**), Requisite #10 Enforcing a Contract (cont'd)

Part 20 (page 32 **JUL 2016**), Requisite #10 Enforcing a Contract (cont'd)

Part 21 (page 24 **SEP 2016**), Enforcing a Contract: the 8th & final question.

Part 22 (page 24 **OCT 2016**), Enforcing a Contract: Step 3 - Impact on your Business.

Part 23 (page 24 **NOV 2016**) Enforcing a Contract: Step 4 - Who to Consult.

Part 24 (page 30 **DEC 2016**): The Role of SLAs - T&Cs - Benefits & Decisions.

Part 25 (page 24 **JAN 2017**): The Role of SLAs - T&Cs - Alternative Dispute Resolutions.

- There is **valuation and certification**: The valuer or certifier makes a ruling based on his own expert knowledge.
- Then there is **negotiation and conciliation**: The parties can resort to negotiation and conciliation with or without the assistance of a third party.
- Thirdly there is **mediation**.
- Lastly, there is **arbitration**.

As indicated in Part 25, the outcome of mediation is not binding on the parties – the mediator expresses an opinion as to what he believes to be a fair and reasonable resolution to the problem. However, the parties can agree to record the finding of the mediator in an agreement which, once accepted and signed by both parties, will be binding and enforceable. The parties can select, failing a satisfactory resolution of their problem via mediation, to proceed to arbitration.

The outcome of arbitration, on the other hand, is binding. Arbitration becomes the method of resolving a dispute if parties to the dispute choose that method of problem-solving at the time, or if it is a clause in an agreement governing the relationship that gave rise to the dispute. The wording of such a clause is of crucial importance and, if poorly worded, it can give rise to many problems e.g. the appointment of the arbitrator, time limits and whether section 20 of the Arbitration Act applies.

Next month (Part 27), I will look at other alternatives and the advantages and disadvantages of Arbitration and Mediation.

Disclaimer: This article is intended to provide a brief overview of legal matters pertaining to the adventure tourism industry and is not intended as legal advice. © Adv Louis Nel, 'Louis The Lawyer', February 2017.

This series of articles explores the legal aspects associated with the risks of operating an adventure tourism business, with specific relevance to the legal framework applicable to South Africa.

Part 8

By 'Louis The Lawyer'

Image courtesy of Canopy Tours

ADVENTURE TOURISM
from a legal perspective

Summary: Part 1 provided definitions for the term Adventure, while Part 2 looked at risk in terms of Nationality of Participant, Service Providers, Bookings, and Terms & Conditions, and Part 3 covered Indemnity and Requirements of the CPA. Part 4 explained why signage must go in hand with a sound indemnity and waiver form, Part 5 dealt with Duty of Care in relation to Negligence, Omission, and Relationship, and Part 6 concluded with Acceptance of Risk and Insurance. Part 7 started the checklist for Risk Identification & Management.

RISK IDENTIFICATION & MANAGEMENT CHECKLIST FOR ADVENTURE SPORT OPERATORS

The issue of confidentiality goes hand in hand with customer information – it is imperative that all operators must have a detailed booking form, which must ideally be completed and signed by the pax and must include reference to and acceptance of the applicable T&C. When dealing with a group (and this is especially common when the activity entails team building), each individual participant must advise his/her age and complete the booking form – if below 18 then the guardian/parent must complete it.

Note that there must in all cases be a separate indemnity (and corresponding signage) – you may have liability related wording in the T&C but each participant must complete and sign an indemnity.

As discussed in earlier articles, all the CPA requirements regarding such an indemnity must be met, failing which enforcing it may become a problem. The comments above regarding groups and the age of participants apply here as well.

It is therefore, imperative that the Business ensures it has a *'healthy relationship'* with the third party service provider (SP) – what does that mean and imply?

You no doubt have certain pax with whom you have established a long-standing relationship and you must ensure that it is honoured by all the SP involved in your *'chain of supply'* – the latter aspect is now underscored by the CPA: at the option of the pax liability is shared by the entire supply chain! You don't not want years of hard work involved in establishing the goodwill and the relationship with your

pax and your brand gets destroyed in a split second by choosing the wrong SP!

How do you choose the right SP? You need to identify and address the potential risks in your relationship and the services to be provided by the SP.

The very first thing you must do (and repeat at least once per year!) is to visit the premises from where the SP provides the activities in question.

You need to establish how well it is managed and how the SP itself establishes and addresses the risks inherent in the activities it provides. This pertains to such matters as staff training, equipment maintenance, indemnity forms and signs, etc. Look for *'tell-tale'* signs.

Make sure that you arrive at the premises well armed with knowledge (knowledge is power) and a detailed checklist – do your homework by making enquiries via organizations e.g. AAXO, ASATA, FGASA, SAACI, SATSA & SITE; visit their website; visit the CIPRO website and find our what you can about their company or close corporation; speak to the industry and get testimonials.

Vehicles and equipment must be properly maintained, insured, meet with statutory requirements, and have logbooks. Do not be shy to ask for records substantiating that and ask probing questions. Have a look for yourself at, for example, the condition of horse riding equipment, quad bikes, canoes, zip line.

Look at the nature of the business, is it a partnership, close corporation or company (see above? This you will have established before your visit, so ask if they have an updated relationship agreement in place. Who are the partners, members or shareholders? 🇹

To be continued in Part 9.

FOOD TOURISM

Are you getting your slice of the pie?

Image courtesy of www.heritage-eastafrica.com

Food tourism is all the rage. Just look at the last decade's vast surge in consumer interest in food and cooking as documented by popular television shows like Iron Chef America and Chopped. There are dozens more examples.

By **Erik Wolf**.

What is food tourism?

At the most basic level, food is a quintessential component of local culture – just like art, music, architecture, film, literature and so on. Unique and memorable food and drink are exciting and even essential components of travel for most people today. Simply put, we define food tourism as the pursuit and enjoyment of unique and memorable food and drink experiences, both far and near.

We say "food tourism," but drinking beverages is an implied and associated activity. It is also cumbersome to say "food and drink tourism." And by "far and near," we mean that in addition to travelling across the country or world for food and beverage experiences, we can also be food travellers in our own regions, cities and neighbourhoods.

If you rarely leave your neighbourhood and travel across town to a new neighbourhood to go to a special grocery store or to eat out, you are also a "food traveller." The distance covered is not as important as the fact that food travellers are explorers and we're always looking for our next unique experience.

You may have heard the terms "culinary tourism," "gastronomy tourism," and even "wine tourism." The World Food Travel Association had previously used the phrase "culinary tourism" to describe our industry. We replaced that phrase with "food tourism" in 2012 because our research indicated that using "culinary" gave a wrong impression. While "culinary" technically can be used for anything relating to food and drink and initially seems to make good sense, the perception among the majority of English-speakers we interviewed is that the word "culinary" is elitist.

Nothing could be further from the truth about what our industry and our Association stand for. "Food Tourism" includes the food carts and street vendors as much as the locals-only (gastro)pubs, dramatic wineries, or one-of-a-kind restaurants.

Food travellers engage in a wide range of activities beyond the feeding of three meals per day. Cooking classes, food tours, wine and beer tastings and even visits to grocery and gourmet stores all rank high on the foodies' to-do list. Food and beverage tourism is about so much more than dining out and wineries.

Even the catering at a corporate event can be considered food tourism if the catering is designed for maximum impact.

Why promote food tourism?

The real value of promoting food tourism is the massive role it plays in driving economic development. We know that visitors spend on average 25% of their travel budget on food and beverages (tax revenue is additional). Without doing expensive, time-consuming research, you can estimate their expenditure for your area if you have data on how much tourists spend overall in your area. Twenty-five percent is significant.

Image courtesy of www.beauchampphotography.com

Food tourism is also an excellent way to foster positive word of mouth. Do you want visitors returning home with memories of chain coffee and hamburgers or do you want them returning as fans raving about the new and different tastes that they experienced? Even better, send them home with stories to share of their culinary experiences in your area, aided by the proliferation of smartphones and the attendant apps like Instagram.

When it comes to measuring food tourism's impact, we also need to look at how much money stays in the local economy. Many tourism marketers look for a spending multiplier. According to the American Independent Business Alliance, chain restaurants recirculate only 34.5% of revenue, while locally-owned restaurants recirculate

65.4%. In other words, money spent in independently owned restaurants is nearly twice as valuable to the community as cash spent in chains, because more of the money stays in the community. Chains have a benefit, namely a predictable meal at a predictable price. The golden egg, however, is when more money stays in our local communities. This is good for local businesses and local governments alike.

Marketing food tourism

Travellers use a wide variety of information resources to help them make the right food and drink choices.

A tourism office is often, but not always, a resource used by visitors. Solid content marketing and a bullet-proof brand message are two tools that should be in your toolbox.

Technology is important too, but it changes rapidly. Have you considered what technology tools are emerging in the next year or two that will help us all reach not just more customers, but also the right customers?

And beyond that, what is coming down the pike for the food tourism industry in general? Have you heard of the Food Tourism 2025 initiative? Incidentally, these forward-looking topics will be covered by industry experts at the biennial FoodTrekking World food

tourism trade convention, which is taking place this April 2-4 in Portland, USA. It's the world's largest gathering of food and beverage tourism professionals.

A restaurant guide that includes global brands that visitors can find on their own does not help them to discover your area's best, nor does it greatly impact your local economy. Why do you think people spend so much time snapping photos of their meals? We're a food-obsessed culture, and thank goodness for that. So, give your visitors what they want. Remember, it's not a meal, it's a memory.

2017 Foodtrekking Awards

Businesses and organizations interested in applying can do so on the Awards website at www.FoodTrekkingAwards.org. Applications are being accepted until February 28, 2017, when the application process will close. Winners will be announced at a special Awards ceremony at FoodTrekking World.

About the author: Erik Wolf is the Executive Director of the World Food Travel Association and the visionary founder of the world's food tourism industry. He is a highly sought speaker, thought leader, strategist and consultant, in the US and abroad, on food and drink tourism issues.

For more info visit www.worldfoodtravel.org

The All-New
MAZDA2 HAZUMI
Auto 1.5L DE

If you're looking for a 'not so little' little car that packs a whole lot of punch, then the Mazda2 Hazumi Auto 1.5L DE is the car for you. I was pleasantly surprised at how spacious and luxurious the interior is – I loved the high quality, crafted feel of the soft-touch leather/cloth combo with its red double-stitching and the 'I'm in charge' feel that the 'cockpit zone' gives, with its push-button keyless start and centre console side panels.

By **Tessa Buhrmann**.

It's actually not surprising that the Mazda2 Hazumi is so easy to love… it was designed with Mazda's *'KODO Soul of Motion Design Language'*, which to quote global design head Ikuo Maedo is to *"express movement with forceful vitality and speed"*. It is said that he also believes that *'an object that receives love and attention from its craftsmen will be given a soul, and that a car is not only a means to go from A to B, but also a reliable partner'*. No wonder I had the compulsion to name the car 'Haz' and take him on a couple of excursions.

I soon got used to the fact that there was no gear lever or clutch in this fabulous subcompact Auto and realised all that I had been missing when it comes to driving in traffic. It's easy to drive in the city and a breeze to park, and the *i-stop* technology (short for idling stop) works like a dream – you simply put your foot on the brake and your engine stops, release the break and you're off again. Technically this speedy restart is due to the fact that the Mazda *i-stop* uses a combustion restart in preference to an electric motor restart. All great for helping with fuel efficiency – in my week of mostly town and suburban driving I averaged 6.5L /100km. Figures of 4.4L / 100km have been quoted, which would very likely be achievable on a long distance trip.

With economy and safety being paramount for most motorists, it was pleasing to know that Mazda's *SKYACTIV* technologies have been adapted for the All-New Mazda2 – this includes the *i-stop* technology, the 6-speed automatic transmission, and *'new generation'* design and materials for both the body and chassis. Despite the lightness of the body, the Madza2 scores high on its collision performance due to a *'multi-load path structure that absorbs and disperses impact force'*. Additionally the Hazumi has dual front airbags, *'smart'* seatbelts and *Dynamic Stability Control*. Other new developments include enhancing performance so as to deliver ease of driving and a good field of vision for the driver.

When the opportunity arose to visit [Tala Collection Private Game Reserve](#) I couldn't refuse. It was great to get the feel of the open road, to test the responsiveness of the *SKYACTIV-Drive* automatic transmission and to make use of the *MZD Connect system* – who wouldn't want to be able to keep tabs on their burgeoning inbox and social networking safely while in the road? Connectivity aside, I was really impressed with the smooth gear changes of the 6-speed automatic transmission and the way the Mazda2 Hazumi handled up hills – especially the twists, turns and incline of Key Ridge on our homeward journey.

One would think that taking a compact 'little' vehicle like the Mazda2 'on safari' would be unwise and perhaps even a little foolish… and I did have my doubts when presented with a map of the conservation reserve and directions to our picnic breakfast! I needn't have worried. Sure I did stay clear of the roads that would have comfortably accommodated the Mazda2's big brother (the Mazda CX-5 2.2 DE Akera FWD), but there were plenty of options for us to enjoy. I was pleasantly surprised by the road clearance and how easy game viewing was – the *i-stop* came in handy for this, and then there was the wonderfully efficient aircon on the way home.

Mazda certainly live up to their marketing blurb with this one. Their aim to "shatter all notions of the subcompact class" is thoroughly executed. I would agree with Mr David Hughes, Managing Director of Mazda Southern Africa when he says *"The All-New Mazda2 condenses the essential DNA of Mazda's new-generation vehicles into a compact car that delivers true motoring value not constrained by conventional notions. In pursuing the ultimate driving experience, we are confident that the Mazda2 delivers a highly responsive performance that South African customers of varying lifestyles can enjoy"*.

To say that I enjoyed driving the Mazda2 Hazumi Auto 1.5L DE would be an understatement! I was sorry to part with my vibrant blue Haz.

But then the Mazda CX-5 2.2L DE Akera AWD MY15 is next up for a Tattler review. I'll have to find another game reserve in KwaZulu-Natal to test drive the CX-5's all-wheel drive capability.

About the author: Tourism Tattler correspondent **Tessa Buhrmann** is the editor of **Responsible Traveller** magazine.
www.responsibletraveller.co.za

FAST FACTS:

All-New Mazda2 Hazumi Auto 1.5L DE

Price:	R294,600 (Incl VAT)
Engine:	1.5 litre in-line 4 cylinder 16 valve DOHC
Compression ratio:	14.8 : 1
Maximum power:	77 kW @ 4,000 rpm
Maximum torque:	250 Nm @ 1,500-2,500 rpm
Fuel:	Diesel
Fuel consumption:	4.4 l/100km (combined)
Air-conditioning:	Climate control
Seat finish:	Half leather seat trim
Navigation :	Satellite
Suspension:	Dynamic Stability Control (DSC)
Warranty:	3-year unlimited kilometre factory warranty
	3-year roadside assistance
	3-year service plan
	5-year Corrosion Warranty.

www.ingramcontent.com/pod-product-compliance
Lightning Source LLC
Chambersburg PA
CBHW041306180526
45172CB00003B/987